ABC

Devotions

26 Practical Lessons
for
Young Christians

Also by Dan Madson

Because I Said So and Other Things Christian Fathers Say

How to do an Ironman in ~~Ten~~ Eleven ~~Easy~~ Difficult Steps: A Lighthearted Look at the Serious Sport of Triathlon and the Ironman Experience

A Woman with a Man Beside Her: Stories for the Better Half

ABC Devotions

ABC

Devotions

26 Practical Lessons
for
Young Christians

Dan Madson

Skrive Publications
Miramar Beach, FL

ISBN 978-1-952037-04-7

Skrive Publications
Miramar Beach, Florida
(608) 332-6986
www.skrivepublications.com

Dedication

This book is dedicated to our six beautiful grandchildren: Sofia, Gianna, Mack, Elia, Jude and Norah.

Introduction

When our kids were growing up, my wife and I were always on the lookout for good reading material for them that was written from a Christian point of view. They attended Christian schools and studied the Bible, the Catechism and other religious books but really didn't have any fun reading material that applied scripture to their daily experiences.

At one point during my teaching career, I was approached by the editor of a Christian periodical to write some articles for young people. I spent several years writing columns that were geared toward kids from grade school through high school.

As our kids got married and started having kids of their own, I decided to revisit one of those series. You can refer to them as devotions, I suppose, but I'll just call them practical lessons based on Bible verses.

I hope that whoever reads this book will enjoy the simple applications that connect Bible verses to real life situations.

I had hoped to compile a month's worth of articles, but I ran out of letters. Plus, I knew that most kids would skip at least four or five days!

$\mathcal{A}$ is for Attitude

Romans 8:28 – And we know that in all things God works for the good of those who love him.

Attitude is everything. I believe you've heard that before. If not from your parents, then from your teachers or your friends. In aviation, the term attitude describes the relationship between an aircraft and the horizon. Is the airplane nose up or nose down? Is it banking right or banking left? The relationship of airplane to horizon is affected mainly by two things: airflow and gravity.

It's not a difficult comparison when talking about a person's attitude in life. Simply put, attitude describes the relationship between a person and his surroundings. Worldly wisdom would have us believe that when good things happen to a person, a good attitude can be expected. Conversely, when bad things happen, a bad attitude is certainly understandable. Is it possible for a person to have bad things happen in his/her life and still have a good attitude?

I know people who have had terrible things happen to them and they are still happy, spirit-filled folks. If questioned about this attitude, they would undoubtedly explain their positive attitudes as nothing more than the outgrowth of their faith in Jesus. No matter what happens to them on this earth, they know they have a place secured in heaven thanks to their Savior Jesus. Once they get there, the glory of that home will render the ills of this world insignificant.

If you have trouble believing Paul's words in Romans "that in all things God works for the good of those who love him" look back at your own life and put those words to the test. The broken right arm you suffered in school before the basketball season? Did it force you to practice with you left hand and thereby become a better all-around player? The broken heart you suffered when your best friend betrayed you? Did it present you with the opportunity to open your heart to a new friend? The broken body of a loved one who died from cancer? Did it sharpen your empathy and make it possible for you to comfort someone else?

It is possible there are things in your life that have not been resolved in a good way...yet. God's good solution, or your understanding of his solution, may not become clear for some time. In fact, it's possible that you won't understand why things happened the way they did until you enter heaven, at which time your conversation with God might go something like this: "Why did you let such terrible things happen to me when I was in 8th grade?"

"For the simple reason that I loved you," God will say. "I tested you in order to strengthen your faith. I wanted you to spend eternity with me."

"What's the most important thing to remember when you're flying an airplane," a child asked a pilot.

"Altitude is everything."

"You mean attitude?"

Yes, that too," the pilot said with a smile.

For the Christian, what is the most important thing

to remember? Trust in Jesus' salvation and in the promise that in all things God works for the good of those who love him. Then a good attitude will be evident to all.

Dear Lord, Please let me have a good attitude today! Help me focus on your love for me and all the good things you have done in my life. In Jesus' name, Amen.

Suggested Bible Reading: Romans 8

My Thoughts

$\mathcal{B}$ is for Beauty

I Corinthians 1:18 – For the message of the cross is foolishness to those who are perishing, but to us who are being saved it is the power of God.

Beauty is in the eye of the beholder. I know it's cliché, but it's true. Our basement flooded a few years ago. Diluted sewage came bubbling up through the drain in the floor and covered the entire basement to a depth of three inches. Carpet was ruined; furniture had to be moved. The smell was less than pleasant. I stood on the stairs with the Roto-Rooter man and looked at the disaster.

To me, it was a horrible sight. To him, it was

beautiful! He made his living fixing messes like mine and seemed happy as a clam to lug his equipment through the murky water and clear the drain.

Ever looked down an old chimney? It's a black, ugly mess to the casual observer. To the chimney sweep, it's a beautiful sight. Ever driven around town after a light snow? Cars are covered with salt and grime. It's depressing for drivers but a beautiful sight to the carwash owners.

Many images in the Bible that Christians hold dear are beautiful to look at—the rainbow God sent after the flood; the angels singing to the shepherds the night Jesus was born; the empty tomb on Easter morning.

Of all the images that remind us of God's love, none stands out more than the Christian cross. It's not that the cross is special in and of itself. It's special because it's the place where God sacrificed his Son to save us from our sins.

I remember seeing *The Passion of the Christ* for the first time. The scene where the Roman soldiers whipped Jesus was so brutal it was difficult to watch. When the soldiers nailed Jesus to the cross, he was nothing but a beaten, bloodied man waiting to die. For those who don't know Jesus as their Savior, it's a horrible sight. To believers, it's the most beautiful image in the world.

When we're troubled by our sins, the cross reminds us that somebody else has already been punished for them. When we're scared about tomorrow, the cross reminds us that our days on earth have already been planned and our future in heaven is a done deal. When we're thankful for the gifts we've been given, it's the image that directs our gratitude to our heavenly Father.

Ever driven past a car dealership after a hailstorm? It's a disaster for the owner, but it will put a smile on the faces of dent repair people all over the city. Remember, beauty is in the eye of the beholder, especially when it comes to the Christian cross.

Dear Lord, Whenever I see a cross, remind me of the beautiful sacrifice your Son made for me. In his name, Amen

Suggested Bible Reading: I Peter 3:3-4

My Thoughts

_____

_____

_____

_____

_____

_____

_____

_____

_____

_____

_____

_____

_____

_____

_____

_____

_____

_____

_____

_____

_____

C is for Character

Galatians 5:22 – The fruit of the Spirit is love, joy, peace, patience, kindness, goodness, gentleness, and self-control.

I would rather *have* character than *be* a character. Let me explain. When I was a kid my dad would sometimes refer to somebody as being a character. Usually that person had done something a little bit naughty or a little bit goofy or said something a little bit strange. I came to view *being* a character as not necessarily a good thing.

Having character is different. Your character, or

the personality traits that define who you are, form the basis for your reputation. Your reputation is valuable. In fact, as a youngster, it might be your most valuable possession.

To demonstrate this to my seventh grade students a few years back, I had each of them determine their net worth. I asked everybody in class to make a list of their possessions and give each item an approximate value. They listed things like clothing, bikes, and video games. Some added up their savings accounts and piggy banks. One kid listed his dog. When they were finished I asked them to add up the total amount of stuff they owned. I asked one student, "So, how much are you worth?"

"If I figured right, about $672," he said.

When Paul wrote this passage to his friends in Galatia, he reminded them that acts of the sinful nature are easy to see. When you're jealous, angry, selfish, stubborn, disobedient, or mean, it's obvious to everybody. If those actions or emotions are repeated often enough, they will form your character. Your character will shape your reputation. Who would want to be remembered as that mean, angry, selfish kid from seventh grade?

It's the same way when you're kind, patient, helpful, joyful, and well-behaved. Those actions and emotions are also easy to observe. As Paul said, they are the fruits of the Spirit. When you were baptized, the Holy Spirit of God created faith in your infant heart. As your body grows, your faith in Jesus will grow too as long as you nourish it properly. Your faith will be demonstrated by your behavior. Wouldn't it be pleasing to be remembered as that kind, patient, helpful, well-behaved kid from seventh grade?

I know a lot of people who *are* characters. I also know a lot of people *with* character. Which would you rather be?

Dear Lord, Help me to *show* character instead of always trying to *be* a character. In Jesus' name, Amen.

Suggested Bible Reading: I Corinthians 15:33

My Thoughts

𝒟 is for Determination

I John 4:10 – This is love: not that we loved God, but that he loved us and sent his Son as an atoning sacrifice for our sins.

Team Hoyt. A son, Rick, born without the ability to walk or talk. A father, Dick, who wanted his son to be like everybody else. Together they have become an inspiration to people all over the world.

Determined to provide a normal life for their son, Dick and his wife enrolled him in public school. Rick learned to write his thoughts using a special computer. When Rick was 15 years old, he communicated to his dad that he wanted to participate in a five-mile benefit run. Dick was not a runner but agreed to push his son in a wheelchair. For the first time in his life, Rick didn't feel handicapped. Today they run marathons. Together they do triathlons. Dick pulls Rick through the water in a small raft. He rides with his son perched on the front of a unique bike. He runs pushing Rick in a specialized wheelchair.

Determined to compete with his son at the highest level, Team Hoyt has completed six Ironman distance triathlons. Dick tows his son through the water for 2.4 miles; he carries him on his bike for another 112; he pushes Rick for 26.2 more miles. Grueling enough for any individual to complete on his own, Dick does it carrying his son.

Determined to show his son the country, Dick trekked 3,770 miles across the United States with Rick. Rick couldn't compete without his dad; Dick wouldn't compete without his son. Dick is the body; Rick is the heart.

It's not always easy to illustrate how deeply God loves you, but Dick Hoyt's example of selfless love and determination paints a pretty good picture.

Your heavenly father took it one step further.

Determined to have an outlet for his infinite love, God created you.

Determined that you would grow to love him, he gave you parents that brought you to the altar of baptism where you were given the gift of faith from the Holy Spirit.

Determined to bring you to heaven someday, God offered his Son to live and die in your place. Your spot in paradise has been reserved. Throughout your life—in good times and bad, through hardship and happiness—God will carry you.

Dear Lord, Help me love you the way I should. I know your love for me is strong and that you are determined to bring me to heaven one day. For that I thank you. In Jesus' name, Amen.

Suggested Bible Reading: I John 4

www.teamhoyt.com

My Thoughts

$\mathcal{E}$ is for Effort

Philippians 3:13-14 - Forgetting what is behind and straining toward what is ahead, I press on toward the goal to win the prize for which God has called me heavenward in Christ Jesus.

Effort is important. I used to tell my students that all the time. I was always puzzled and frustrated by gifted students or athletes that didn't try very hard. On the other hand, kids who weren't that talented but worked hard to achieve success always inspired me. They didn't always get A's and

B's on their report cards, but they sure studied hard. They weren't always starters on the basketball team, but they practiced their tails off. Given the choice between working with one kind of student or the other, I would take the latter any day.

Growing as a Christian takes effort. Your salvation is signed, sealed, and delivered. No amount of effort could earn you a place in heaven. But your life of sanctification is a different story. In order to put your life in line with God's will, you have to think about it all the time. And you have to do things that will strengthen your faith.

It takes effort to get to church on a weekly basis. This is where you hear the two things that you need to hear all the time. One, you're a worthless sinner. Two, you have a Savior who loves you and gave his life for you. Your sins have been taken away and you have a place in heaven reserved. These days, most churches offer multiple worship opportunities. If you can't worship on Sunday morning, you can attend services on a different day.

It takes effort to keep God's word in your life on a daily basis. Think of all the distractions that seem so important like TV shows, phone conversations, jobs or sleep. What could be more important than five or ten quiet minutes in the morning or in the evening reading God's word or an inspiring chapter from a book based on God's word? Or one of these devotions?

It takes effort to let your light shine in the community. I bet there's a senior citizen in your neighborhood that would enjoy some company once in a while. I bet your boss would appreciate it if you did a little extra on the job each day. I bet your parents would love it if you helped out around the house once in a while.

Effort is important. Like Paul, let's strain toward what is ahead and press on!

Dear Lord, Forgive me for the times when I don't try very hard. Help me show strong effort in all the tasks I do each day. In Jesus' name, Amen.

●●

Suggested Bible Reading: Philippians 3

My Thoughts

_____

_____

_____

_____

_____

_____

_____

_____

_____

_____

_____

_____

_____

_____

_____

_____

_____

_____

_____

_____

_____

$\mathcal{F}$ is for Forbidden

1 Corinthians 10:13 - No temptation
has seized you except what is common
to man. And God is faithful; he will not
let you be tempted beyond what you
can bear. But when you are tempted, he
will also provide a way out so that
you can stand up under it.

Forbidden Fruits Create Many Jams! Driving
down the highway recently, I saw those words on

a sign. At first I thought it was a cute saying advertising products to spread on toast. Then it dawned on me. The sign was in front of a church and the words were a subtle reminder about what happens when we do things we shouldn't.

Adam and Eve found out the hard way. After disobeying God's command not to eat the fruit of a certain tree in the Garden of Eden, the couple found themselves in trouble up to their eyeballs. In an effort to escape responsibility for this first sin, they tried to hide. They started lying. Eve blamed the serpent. Adam blamed Eve. In the end, they had to face up to what they had done and suffer the chilling consequences.

Later on, God set specific boundaries for his people to keep them from getting into jams. These were commandments, mind you, not suggestions. Don't be disobedient, don't kill, don't lust, don't steal, don't swear, and don't covet.

Forbidden fruits are everywhere. Tomorrow when you wake up you will be bombarded with temptations to do all sorts of things you're not supposed to do. Is it possible to avoid sinning? Sadly, no. Because of your inborn human nature, you will never be free from the temptation to sin.

However, there is some good news to balance the bad. Read the passage above. Do you understand what it means? God allows temptations in your life to test your faith and to give you a chance to demonstrate your love for him. When faced with any temptation, you always have two choices – to sin or not to sin. God will never allow you to be put in a situation where your only choice is to commit a sin.

When you fail a test, commit a sin, and get yourself into a jam, God will forgive you upon repentance. When you pass a test and avoid sin, God will be truly happy. *Forbidden fruits create many jams*. Remember the warning, and be happy that a loving Savior forgives your sins.

Dear Lord, When I'm tempted to sin today, help me make the choice that pleases you. In Jesus' name, Amen.

Suggested Bible Reading: Genesis 3

My Thoughts

_____

_____

_____

_____

_____

_____

_____

_____

_____

_____

_____

_____

_____

_____

_____

_____

_____

_____

_____

_____

_____

_____

$\mathcal{G}$ is for Google

John 20:31 - But these are written that you may believe that Jesus is the Christ, the Son of God, and that by believing you may have life in his name.

Google. What a funny word. Say it a few times. Google. Google. Google, Google, Google! See what I mean? Want to find out what time a movie starts? Google it! Want to learn about the building of the Panama Canal? Google it! Want a good recipe for baked salmon? Google it!

You know you've done well when something you

have created becomes a household name. The person or persons who developed the Google search engine have turned a funny word into a billion dollar business. Its sole purpose is to satisfy our insatiable appetite for information. There's only one problem. How do you know that the information provided by a Google search is accurate? Who checks the facts? Who verifies the truth?

As a young Christian, I know you have questions that beg for answers. I'm not talking about questions that can be Googled. I'm talking about serious spiritual questions. How is it possible for a baby to come to faith? How can God keep loving me when I sin so much? What is my purpose in life? Is there really a heaven and am I really going there if I believe in Jesus?

The answers to spiritual questions can all be found in one source—the Bible. How do you know that the information recorded in the Bible is true? Because God himself wrote it. The same God who called the universe into existence by merely speaking. The same God who raised up a chosen people to call his own. The same God who sent his only Son to suffer and die in your place. In II Peter it says "men spoke from God as they were carried along by the Holy Spirit." God breathed into the minds of the writers of the Bible the very words he wanted them to write, thereby assuring us that every word is true.

John 20:31 comes at the end of an interesting chapter. After his resurrection, Jesus appeared a number of times to his followers. Many of them had questions about his fate that needed answering. John tells us that Jesus did many miraculous signs in the presence of his disciples. He did so many, in fact, that it was impossible for John to write them all down. He concluded by writing verse 31 that appears under the title of the article.

"But *these* are written that you may believe..." That phrase sums up the entire Bible. There are parts of the Bible that are difficult to understand. However, the simple truth of God's love for sinners is easy enough for anybody to grasp.

Want to learn about the Battle at Gettysburg? Google it! Want to know what time the Super Bowl starts? Google it! When you want answers to spiritual questions, refer to the only source of absolute truth—the Bible.

Dear Lord, Help me stay focused today on the information that is most important for me – that Jesus loves me and has saved me from my sins. In His name, Amen.

Suggested Bible Reading: John 20

My Thoughts

$\mathcal{H}$ is for Hope

Romans 12:12 - Be joyful in hope.

"I hope I get a good grade on my test tomorrow," my son said once when he was in my 7th grade class.

"Did you study?" I asked him.

"Not much," he said.

"Well, there's really not much hope then, is there?"

"Probably not," he admitted.

Hope is a word or idea that has subtle differences in meaning. Hope can be a wish that something will happen (I hope my wife changes her mind and lets me go skydiving). Hope can refer to a chance that something desirable will happen (I hope it keeps raining so I don't have to mow the lawn today).

For the Christian, hope is a *confident desire*. God has made some amazing promises. He has told us He will never leave us or forsake us. He has made it clear that He will forgive all our sins through faith in Jesus' death on the cross. Best of all, He has promised that we will go to heaven when we die and will share in all the glories that await us there.

Christianity is unique in that it is the only major religion in the world that does not teach salvation by works. Think of all the people in the world who are trying to earn their way to heaven by being good. It must be stressful for such people, wondering all the time if they have done enough good things to earn God's love. Their hope is tied up in a futile effort to be good enough, or at least to be better than others.

When you read Paul's letter to Christians in Rome long ago, he ably described how Christians should live—not to earn God's favor but to thank Him for salvation: Share; be devoted to each other; bless and do not curse; practice hospitality; do not be conceited; hate what is evil; *be joyful in hope*.

The hope Paul referred to is the same hope shared by modern Christians. When you wake up each day, you never have to think, "I wonder if God loves me." He does! He created you, gifted you with faith, and set you apart as one of His own children. You never have to think, "I hope God can forgive what I did yesterday." He already has! God sent His own Son to be nailed to the cross in order to pay for your sins. You never have to think, "I wonder if there really is a heaven." There is! Scripture is full of descriptions of heaven and Jesus has prepared a place just for you, as he himself said in John 14:1-6.

Be joyful in hope—not the wishful kind of hope, but the confident hope that Christians share. Remember: "Your hope is built on nothing less than Jesus' blood and righteousness" (ELH #197).

Dear Lord, Whenever I have doubts about my salvation, remind me that my hope is a confident desire. Help me live in that confidence today. In Jesus' name, Amen.

Suggested Bible Reading: Romans 12

My Thoughts

_____

_____

_____

_____

_____

_____

_____

_____

_____

_____

_____

_____

_____

_____

_____

_____

_____

_____

_____

_____

_____

I is for Ignorance

Romans 10:17 - Faith comes from hearing the message, and the message is heard through the word of Christ.

A few years ago at a high school basketball game one of my 7th grade students came up to me at half time with a hotdog in each hand. Half of one was already in her mouth, and she was chewing it with a smile on her face. To tease her I said, "Do you have any idea what goes into making a hotdog?"

"No," she said. "What?"

"Ah. Ignorance is bliss," I said.

"What does that mean?" she said.

"You just explained it," I said. She walked away perplexed.

There are things in this world that young people don't need to know – things that eventually will become evident. Our government is often corrupt. It's hard being a parent. There are indeed 230 calories in a half-cup of ice cream.

On the other hand, there are things young Christians can't afford *not* to know. How did God create me and bring me to faith? What am I supposed to do with my life? How am I going to get to heaven? The answers to these questions are found in the scriptures. The fact you are reading this article leads me to believe that you already know the answers to those questions.

It's more than likely that you have been reared by Christian parents, brought to faith through the miracle of baptism, and received Biblical instruction from Christian pastors or teachers. They are fulfilling a Biblical directive to perpetuate the kingdom of Jesus Christ here on this earth. They are also preparing you for eternity. Your parents and your pastors and teachers did not want you to grow up ignorant of the truths of the Bible.

That's a good thing because on the Day of Judgment, ignorance will not be an acceptable excuse for being unprepared to meet your Maker. I know that sounds unfair, but it's true. Furthermore, it places a responsibility on you as a young Christian to do your part to bring the truths of the Bible to others.

In Romans 10, Paul the Apostle wrote, "Everyone who calls on the name of the Lord will be saved." He anticipated the question that this statement might bring out. "What if someone doesn't know of the Lord? Then what?"

Paul continued by saying, "How, then, can they call on the one they have not believed in? And how can they believe in the one of whom they have not heard? And how can they hear without someone preaching to them? Consequently, faith comes from hearing the message, and the message is heard through the word of Christ." In essence, he was telling his readers that they were to bring this message to others.

Ignorance is bliss...in some cases. When it comes to your spiritual life, ignorance is dangerous. Your Savior wants you to share eternity in heaven with him one day. He has already done everything necessary to make that possible. Since faith comes from hearing the message, get ready to share that message with others!

Dear Lord, I don't want to be ignorant of your Word. Make me a better student so I can share your Word with others. In Jesus' name, Amen.

****

Suggested Bible Reading: Romans 10:13-15

My Thoughts

J is for Jesus

Matthew 27:22 - Pilate asked, "What shall I do, then, with Jesus?"

Before he was born, Jesus created a stir. Prophets made predictions about him. Faithless nations despised him. His chosen people looked forward to his appearance. His parents planned for him.

What are *you* going to do with Jesus?

From the day of his birth, Jesus created a stir. Shepherds hastened to find him. Wise men traveled to worship him. King Herod tried to kill him. Aged believers longed to hold him. Teachers in the temple sat and listened to him. Grown men quit their jobs to follow him. Friends loved him. Crowds of listeners were amazed by him. Satan tempted him. His Father was pleased with him. His rivals were jealous of him. Pilate was puzzled by him. His enemies finally killed him.

What are *you* going to do with Jesus?

He is the Alpha and the Omega, the Beginning and the End. He is the Firstborn over all Creation and the Heir of all Things. He is the Image of God and the Ruler of God's Creation. He is the Lord of Glory, the Lord of Lords, the Lord of All. He is I Am!

What are *you* going to do with Jesus?

He is the Last Adam. He is the Son of God and the Son of Man. He is the Root and Offspring of David. He is the Lion of the Tribe of Judah. He is the Chief Cornerstone, the Bridegroom, the Faithful Witness to All that is True. He is Immanuel!

What are *you* going to do with Jesus?

He is the Gate. He is the Way, the Truth, and the Life! He is Holy and True, the Hope of Glory and the Horn of Salvation. He is the Light of the World.

He is the King of Israel, the King of the Ages, the King Eternal!

What are *you* going to do with Jesus?

He is our Protection, our Redemption, our Righteousness, our Sacrificed Passover Lamb, the Lamb without Blemish. He is the True Bread, the True Light, and the True Vine. He simply is Truth!

What are *you* going to do with Jesus?

He is our Rock, our Word, our Prophet, our Great High Priest. He is our Mediator and the Judge of the Living and the Dead. He is the Head of the Church. He is the Atoning Sacrifice for our Sin. He is our Hope of Glory!

What are *you* going to do with Jesus?

Today, 2,000 years after his death, Jesus is still creating a stir. People still build churches for him. Unbelievers still mock him. His followers still pray to him and wait for his return. His Father still has him seated him at the right hand of the throne of glory. The angels still serve him.

What are *you* going to do with Jesus?

Dear Jesus, I know who you are! You are my Savior and my friend. Stay by my side today and every day. In your name I pray, Amen.

●●●

Suggested Bible Reading: Luke 2

My Thoughts

_____
_____
_____
_____
_____
_____
_____
_____
_____
_____
_____
_____
_____
_____
_____
_____
_____
_____
_____
_____
_____

K is for Karma

Galatians 6:7 - Do not be deceived: God cannot be mocked. A man reaps what he sows.

There was a silly sit-com on the air a few years back called *My Name is Earl*. The main character was a happy-go-lucky goofball named Earl Hickey. After finding a winning lottery ticket worth $100,000 in the middle of the street, he lets out a holler and immediately gets hit by a car.

He determines that this misfortune was payback for all the bad things he had done in his life. He proceeds to make a list of those things and sets out to rectify them all. During each episode Earl crosses one item off his list. "Karma is a funny thing," he says.

Karma is not a Christian concept. It is a well-known philosophy of eastern religions like Buddhism and Hinduism. Essentially the law of karma states, "If you do good things, good things will happen to you; if you do bad things, bad things will happen to you." In the time it took you to read this paragraph, you may have already figured out a couple of flaws in the law of karma.

First of all, bad things happen to God's people all the time. Car accidents claim the lives of innocent passengers. Cancer strikes unsuspecting victims. Families are divided by divorce. God allows bad things to happen to his people for a reason. It may be to strengthen their faith; it may be to draw them closer to him; it may be to help somebody else who is going through a similar struggle. In some cases we won't know why something happened until we get to heaven. Rest assured, however, that for people who love God, all things will work for good.

Secondly, good things happen to ungodly people all the time. Writers who defy the existence of God sell truckloads of books. Entertainers earn millions of dollars producing vile music and movies and then flaunt their lavish lifestyles for all to see. Unethical business people run huge companies. God, by his very nature, is generous. His goodness spills over into the laps of ungodly people, but sin and unbelief have consequences.

Paul warned the Galatians: "Do not be deceived: God cannot be mocked. A man reaps what he sows. The one who sows to please his sinful nature, from that nature will reap destruction; the one who sows to please the Spirit, from the Spirit will reap eternal life."

Karma? I don't think so. More like sin and grace. We are all sinners who deserve nothing but bad things, including eternal destruction. Yet we have a substitute, a Savior who has taken away every one of our sins by virtue of his perfect life and his death on the cross. Now that would make a good show!

Dear Lord, Even when bad things happen to me, I know you love me and are preparing me for heaven. Keep me grounded in my simple Christian faith today and always. In Jesus' name, Amen.

Suggested Bible Reading: Galatians 6:7-10

My Thoughts

L is for Love

1 John 3:16 – This is how we know what love is: Jesus Christ laid down his life for us. And we ought to lay down our lives for our brothers.

My wife's 91-year-old father passed away last year. After her mother died seven years ago, she tried to call her dad every day to talk to him. At the end of every conversation, she always said, "I love you, Dad."

"I love you too," he would respond.

Those three words pass my wife's lips frequently.

Our three adult children, their spouses and our six grandchildren hear them all the time. Her friends hear them all the time, and so do I. Honestly, I never get tired of hearing that somebody loves me.

1 John 3 is a great section of the Bible to read if you want to understand love. Verse 16 (above) defines God's love for you. He created you out of love and then made the ultimate sacrifice by sending his Son Jesus to die for you. In response, the writer says you ought to lay down your life for your brother. That's a romantic notion, but can any modern-day Christian hope to make that sacrifice? Perhaps not, but there are other ways to demonstrate that you understand and appreciate God's love.

First of all, stop sinning. And by that I mean, stop sinning. Seriously, I'm not kidding! Stop sinning! It's true you were born infected with original sin, and it's true you live in a sinful world. However, every morning when you wake up you have a new chance to avoid temptation. Every day you have a new chance to stand clear of the pet sins with which you struggle. Every day you have another chance to plunge your spirit into the waters of your baptism and emerge a cleansed and forgiven child of God.

Secondly, love each other. And by each other I mean your family members, your neighbors, your friends, your teachers, and even people who don't love you back. It's OK to save the words 'I love you' for people in your life who are closest to you. For others, it's possible to love with actions and truth.

Every day you have hundreds of chances to perform simple, selfless acts of love for others. Make your bed in the morning. Clean up the kitchen table after breakfast. Do a load of your own laundry. Help a classmate with an assignment. Tell a teacher you appreciate his or her teaching style. Be a good listener. Obey those in authority. Say thank-you when somebody does something nice for you. Pray.

My wife just got off the phone with our daughter. Guess what she told her before she hung up?

Dear Lord, Help me show love today. Not just to my family and friends but to all with whom I come in contact. In Jesus' name, Amen.

Suggested Bible Reading: I John 3

My Thoughts

M is for Moderation

II Corinthians 9:6 – Whoever sows sparingly will reap sparingly, and whoever sows generously will also reap generously.

Competitive eating? Can you stomach (no pun intended) watching a 430-pound man sit behind a table piled with food and, under the watchful eye of a judge, stuff as much of it into his mouth as possible in 10 minutes?

Ultimate fighting? Do you have the nerve to watch two muscular brawlers bouncing around on a blood stained canvas pounding each other senseless until one submits to the other?

Our culture is filled with examples of extreme, immoderate behavior. Much of it is violent; most of it is unappetizing.

Paul's 2nd letter to the Corinthians offers some advice to Christians about moderate living. In most cases 'everything in moderation' is a good creed by which you can live. Paul suggests one time when it's good to be immoderate, and it has to do with giving.

In v. 7, Paul continues: *Each man should give what he has decided in his heart to give, not reluctantly or under compulsion, for God loves a cheerful giver.* God knows a thing or two about giving. He brought you to life and gave you faith. He gives you daily blessings that are too numerous to count. *He has scattered abroad his gifts to the poor; his righteousness endures forever.*

Above all, he has given you a Savior from sin. That gift alone is all the motivation you need to give back to God. One of the best ways to give back to God is to give to other people. Paul continues in v. 11: *You will be made rich in every way so that you can be generous on every occasion, and through us your generosity will result in thanksgiving to God.*

Each of you has been made rich in various ways. You have unique personality traits and special skills. You have time, money and ideas to share. *This service that you perform is not only supplying the needs of God's people but is also overflowing in many expressions of thanks to God.*

Base jumping? Would you be willing to take the plunge from the top of a 100-story skyscraper?

Immoderate living has become acceptable, often celebrated, in our modern world. As a Christian young person, remember that moderation is usually a good principle to follow except when it comes to giving back to God.

Dear Lord, Help me to practice moderation today, except when it comes to giving to others. In Jesus' name, Amen.

Suggested Bible Reading: II Corinthians 9

My Thoughts

N is for Now

II Corinthians 6:2 - Now is the time of God's favor, now is the day of salvation.

When I was in college I had a sign above my desk that said, "The sooner you fall behind, the more time you have to catch up." I lived by that motto and didn't always use my time in the best manner. More than once I sat down after midnight to write a ten-page paper that was due at 8:00 o'clock the next morning. It seemed like there were so many other fun things to do instead of schoolwork.

God has never had trouble with procrastination.

Granted, his understanding of time is different than ours. He is not constrained by clocks or calendars. My father used to explain it like this: "Imagine a pile of wheat a mile high, a mile wide, and a mile deep. Every 10,000 years a bird flies by and picks up one grain of wheat. When the entire pile is gone, it would be like a minute of God's existence."

Throughout history, God has always done the right thing at exactly the right time. When it pleased him, he brought the universe into existence by speaking his omnipotent word.

When the fullness of time had come (in other words, at the perfect moment in history), God sent his son Jesus into the world to suffer and die for all our sins.

More recently, when the time was right, *you* were born and brought to faith through baptism. Many of you have been confirmed or graduated from high school...all when God wanted it to happen.

In the Bible verse above, Paul urge his listeners to be concerned about right now. Why? Right now is an important time in your life. Right now God is loving you and listening to you. Right now God is thinking about you and making plans for you. Right now, God is offering you forgiveness, comfort, peace, and strength.

If you occasionally procrastinate when it comes to your schoolwork or chores around the house, no big deal. Like me, some of you may work better under pressure. However, when it comes to your faith and Christian living, don't put things off that you should do right now. Stay in touch with God through personal prayer. Be mindful of the needs of fellow believers. Do things that will strengthen your faith.

One day in the future at precisely the right time, Jesus will come again. Keep your hearts and minds ready for that wonderful day. *Now* is the time of God's favor! *Now* is the day of salvation!

Dear Lord, Help me to not be a procrastinator today, especially when it comes to the needs of others. In Jesus' name, Amen.

Suggested Bible Reading: Psalm 118

My Thoughts

O is for Omnipotent

Hebrews 1:3 - The Son is the radiance of God's glory and the exact representation of his being, sustaining all things by his powerful word.

I have always liked odd words like *onomatopoeia*. *Onomatopoeia* refers to a word that sounds like its meaning. Say the word *cuckoo* in a singsong voice. Whisper the word *silence*. Stand up with your arms outstretched, tilt your head back and boom out the word *omnipotent*! Do you get it?

I learned the words omnipotent, omniscient, and

omnipresent from my dad in confirmation class. I felt pretty smart knowing the meaning of each of those words.

When I was teaching 7th grade myself, I recall a lively discussion among my students about which attribute they would most like to have. Almost without exception, the kids in my class thought it would be the most fun to be omnipotent. They agreed it would be cool to know all things and to have the ability to be present in all places at the same time. But to be all-powerful? That would be awesome!

I reminded them that along with omnipotence would come tremendous responsibility. To illustrate what I meant, I had them look out the window at some of the cars in the parking lot. Many of them were beat up rust buckets on wheels. At one time each owner had the power to purchase a brand new vehicle, but none of them had the ability to keep it looking and running like new.

When God created the universe, he didn't have a crew of construction workers running here and there. He made simple, exact pronouncements like, "Let there be light" and "Let us make man in our image." The only tool he used was his holy and omnipotent word. God's original creation was so dramatically beautiful and so full of interesting creatures that we can only imagine what it must have been like.

Adam and Eve's sin ruined what was meant to remain perfect. Undeterred, God sent his son into the world to fix what was broken and to redeem us from sin. He exalted Jesus to his right hand where he sustains the creation even today.

Cracks have appeared in God's handiwork because of man's sinfulness. Nations war. Natural disasters wreak havoc on our planet. Economies flounder. The human condition becomes more depraved. But don't be fooled, God's omnipotent word will exist forever, and his Son will continue to sustain all things through that word.

Buzz. Squeak. Mumble. Omnipotent! All are good examples of *onomatopoeia*. I'm glad God has all that power. I don't think anybody else could handle the responsibility.

Dear Lord, Thank you for creating the whole universe. Thank you for creating me. Help me serve you today knowing that you love me as your dear child. In Jesus' name, Amen.

•••

Suggested Bible Reading: Genesis 1

My Thoughts

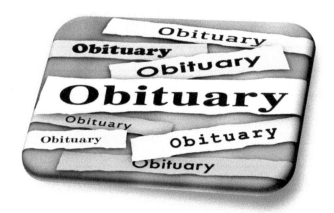

P is for Posthumous

Matthew 5:12 - Rejoice and be glad, because great is your reward in heaven.

Have you read any obituaries lately? If so, you may have noticed that each person whose obituary appears in your local paper never did anything wrong. Each was the most virtuous, loving person ever born. Each was the best athlete, the hardest worker, and the most dedicated outdoorsman known to mankind. Each was a paragon of virtue who should have been knighted, sainted, or at least voted into the local hall of fame.

"Robert S., husband and father, passed from this

life to his eternal rest on January 4th, 2008. Robert was married to his wife for 28 years. He was a loving and faithful husband. He was the best dad ever to his three children. His neighbors always counted on him to fix things that broke. He loved the outdoors and his three dogs will miss him as much as his friends. He was a hard working leader at his company and loved by all his coworkers." Sound familiar?

I'm not trying to poke fun of somebody who has died, but I'd be interested in hearing the real story. It might read something like this:

"Robert S., husband and father, is finally gone! Thank goodness! His wife got tired of making all his meals and picking up after him every day without so much as a 'thank-you.' He yelled at his kids all the time. His neighbors were sick and tired of the fact that he never mowed his lawn because he was always off hunting or fishing with his three dogs. His coworkers tolerated him because he was the son of the company's founder."

I realize that obituaries are meant to celebrate, not defame, the life of a person. As Christians, however, we can read between the accolades. No matter how wonderful a person is made out to be posthumously, Christians understand the truth.

All people are born with original sin. All people spend their lives sinning continually. All people need a Savior.

When I die, I'd like my obituary to be simple: "Dan Madson - He lived in sin; he died in faith; he resides in heaven."

Dear Lord, Help me see the best in others today even as I ask that they see the best in me! In Jesus' name, Amen.

Suggested Bible Reading: Matthew 5: 43-48

My Thoughts

Q is for Quiet

Isaiah 30:15 - This is what the Lord, says: "In repentance and rest is your salvation, in quietness and trust is your strength."

I have very sensitive ears. I'm not sure if it's a blessing or a curse. My family loves watching TV with the volume blaring. The first thing I do when I walk into the family room is grab the remote and dial down the noise. "Hey!" everybody yells. "We can't hear the TV!"

"I can hear it clear as a bell, and I was outside across the street! It's too loud."

"Dad, your ears are super sensitive. Are you sure you're not a bat?"

We live in a noisy world. From the minute we get up in the morning until the time we go to bed, our senses are bombarded with a cacophony of sound. Cars, trucks, and motorcycles driving around, airplanes flying overhead, loud music and louder TV commercials blasting, people talking, laughing, and yelling. The list is endless. I challenge you to think of the last time you remember being aware of absolute quiet. It happened to me a few years ago.

We were in the panhandle of Florida nervously watching the path of the latest hurricane as it tracked its way toward the United States. The night before we were supposed to begin feeling the effects of the outer edge of the storm, we had a brief power outage around the building in which we were staying. My wife and I were standing on the balcony that overlooks the Gulf of Mexico. Suddenly, all the lights in and around our neighborhood blinked out. The Gulf was flat calm, water black as ink, the proverbial calm before the storm. Not a single car drove by. The few people that we could see walking along the water stopped and looked around, silhouetted in the moonlight.

There was not a breath of wind. We stood on the balcony in absolute darkness and quietness. We looked at each other and my wife said, "This is really creepy."

"I think it's awesome," I said. For a full twenty minutes we were surrounded by complete silence and darkness before power was restored.

God wants his people to be quiet once in a while. What better time to do that than on Sunday morning at church? After a week of working, playing, and studying, I can't think of a better place to spend an hour in relative peace and quiet than in church.

Isaiah wrote, *"In repentance and rest is your salvation, in quietness and trust is your strength."* I look forward each week to that hour of rest and quietness. During that weekly hour I know I will hear two important things: I'm a sinner who needs to repent, and I have a Savior who has guaranteed my salvation through his life, death, and resurrection.

When you grow tired of all the noise surrounding you, retire to your church for an hour where you can rest, repent, and reflect. And turn down the TV. I can hear it from here.

Dear Lord, Help me be a good listener today. There's so much noise in the world. Keep me focused on your words and promises. In Jesus' name, Amen.

●●●●●●●●●●●●●●●●●●●●●●●●●●●●●●●●●●●●●

Suggested Bible Reading: Mark 6: 30-44

My Thoughts

R is for Rescue

Genesis 3:15 – "I will put enmity between you and the woman, and between your offspring and hers; he will crush your head, and you will strike his heel."

They called it the *Great Rescue*. Millions of risky home loans were given to unqualified borrowers. When home values dropped and interest rates increased, many of those people were unable to make their payments and defaulted on their loans. As a result, powerful financial institutions that had built business on these shaky loans went bankrupt.

Greedy executives walked away from these failed companies with millions of dollars. Shareholders lost everything. Wall Street faced an impending disaster.

The solution? Our nation's political leaders gathered in Washington D.C. to hammer out an agreement. In the end, Congress passed a law that provided more than $700 billion dollars of taxpayer money to bail out the offenders and boost a struggling economy. Taxes that had been collected for government programs were sent back to the very people who helped cause the problem in the first place. Some rescue.

Every year when Christians prepare for the Christmas and Easter seasons, we can ponder and appreciate the greatest rescue in history. Genesis 3:15 is the first recorded promise of a Savior. It set God's rescue plan into motion.

After the creation, God intended that mankind would live in perfect harmony with him. When Adam and Eve fell into sin, everything changed. However, instead of destroying his supreme creatures, God provided hope for Adam and Eve and all mankind when he told the devil that a Savior was coming who would crush his power. He set a rescue plan in motion.

The plan was costly. $700 billion dollars would

pale in comparison. At just the right time in the world's history, God sent his own dear son to this earth to rescue sinners. Jesus was born into poverty. He grew to adulthood like anybody else. He was tempted continually and never once fell into sin. When he began his preaching ministry, those who hated him challenged him at every turn. In the end, his enemies captured him, tortured him, and hung him on a cross to die.

Before he breathed his final breath, Jesus claimed victory. When he said, "It is finished!" he meant that the greatest rescue in history had finally been completed.

As God's people, we are now free from sin. We have direct access to God the Father through Jesus. We have a place in heaven secured for us. Now that's what I call a Great Rescue!

Dear Lord, Thank you for rescuing me from sin, death and the power of the devil. In Jesus' name, Amen.

Suggested Bible Reading: John 19:30

My Thoughts

S is for Stupidity

Ecclesiastes 7:25 - I turned my mind to search out wisdom and to understand the stupidity of wickedness and the madness of folly.

Is the gap between wisdom and stupidity widening? You be the judge. With movies, TV shows, and entire websites devoted to people doing stupid things, it's not difficult to find plenty of examples.

A teenage boy, in a foolish attempt to skateboard down a railing the length of two flights of stairs, falls and fractures his right leg, breaks four ribs and cracks his skull. A curious visitor at a New York zoo sneaks into a polar bear's cage and is mauled to death by the bear. The mother of a high school cheerleader, jealous that her daughter was overlooked for a spot on the cheer team, hires a hit-man to kill the mother of her daughter's rival.

There is a fine line between wicked stupidity and ignorant foolishness. Both, however, are distinctly different from wisdom, especially the wisdom referred to in the passage above.

The writer of the book of Ecclesiastes is not identified in the Bible, but several passages suggest that King Solomon is the author. In any case, the writer of the book developed a clear, simple theme throughout its 12 chapters: Life not centered on God is purposeless and meaningless. Without him, nothing can satisfy. With him, all of life and all of his good gifts are to be gratefully received.

The seventh chapter of Ecclesiastes is titled 'Wisdom.'

Consider some…

"A good name is better than fine perfume."

"It is better to heed a wise man's rebuke than to listen to the song of fools."

"Patience is better than pride."

"Do not be quickly provoked, for anger resides in the lap of fools."

"When times are good, be happy; but when times are bad, consider: God has made the one as well as the other."

"The man who fears God will avoid all extremes."

"There is not a righteous man on earth who does what is right and never sins."

Like everything else in this world, wisdom pursued by sinful people will always fall short of God's standard of perfection. By faith, God's people understand and accept this limitation and can enjoy life as God gives it.

So, avoid stupidity. Live carefully. Be prudent in everything. Fear God, and keep his commandments.

Dear Lord, When I do stupid things, forgive me. Help me to live according to your rules today. Give me the wisdom to do what is right. In Jesus' name, Amen.

Suggested Bible Reading: James 1:22-25

My Thoughts

T is for Temptation

Matthew 6:13 - And lead us not into temptation, but deliver us from the evil one.

As an experienced sinner, allow me to explain the anatomy of a sin. First, the devil will tempt you with the thought of doing something contrary to God's commands. It could be just about anything, but often it will relate to a specific weakness that he knows you have. Then, he will try to convince you that doing something wrong isn't that big a deal. He will persistently appeal to your greed or your stubbornness, your laziness or your lust. If you fall into sin, he will dull your conscience or try

81

to convince you that you have done something terrible—something that God could never forgive.

Every day you will be tempted many, many times. Some of the temptations will be subtle and fleeting. Others will be overt and difficult to ignore. Some will be so overwhelming that you may feel there is no option but to give in and commit the sin. I'm here to remind you of one of the coolest promises in all of Scripture. God will never cause you to sin. He will allow you to be tempted, but you will never be put into a situation where your only choice is to commit a sin. That's great news!

The Bible offers countless examples of people who were tempted to sin. Some gave in; some didn't. Two examples will be sufficient to explain the passage above:

JUDAS – Satan identified Judas' weakness for money and tempted him to betray his Savior with the promise of a pocket full of silver coins. He convinced Judas that it was no big deal to conspire with Jesus' enemies. They would eventually catch up with him anyway. Once the deal was done, however, Satan changed his tune. He tortured Judas with the idea that what he had done was so terrible that there was no chance he could be forgiven. Tragically, Judas perished without that blessed forgiveness even though it would have been granted had he repented.

JESUS – Satan tried his best to lead Jesus into sin. He personally tempted Jesus with some very attractive sins. Again, he made it sound like disobeying God was not a big deal. The difference between Judas and Jesus is that Jesus understood how to overcome each temptation. He used his knowledge of the word of God and let the love that he had for his heavenly Father rule his heart and influence his decisions.

Each of you can do the same when you are tempted to sin. Use your knowledge of God's word. Lean on the promises that he has made to you, including the one in the passage above. And when you do succumb to temptation? Humble yourself, tell God you are sorry, and accept his unending offer of forgiveness.

Dear Lord, Give me strength today to overcome temptation. If I fall into sin, forgive me for the sake of your Son. In His name, Amen.

Suggested Bible Reading: II Samuel 11 and 12

My Thoughts

U is for Uncertainty

Proverbs 3:5 – Trust in the Lord with all your heart and lean not on your own understanding.

Dear Jesus,

I usually don't worry much, but I've been nervous about a few things lately. It seems like our country is falling apart. Everybody is angry with everybody else. Nobody can agree on anything. My dad is getting older and misses my mom. My wife's mom and dad are both gone, and I know she misses them terribly. I worry about our kids and their jobs. I worry about our grandchildren as they grow up in a world of uncertainty. My left knee and left shoulder hurt all the time and even my back is starting to give me trouble. I try to stay positive, but it's not easy. I thought it might help to write you a letter and ask for some advice.

Sincerely, Daniel Madson

Dear Dan,

Thanks for the note. First off, I know your last name, so Dan will be fine as a closing. I don't get too many paper letters anymore, what with email so popular these days. I'm glad you wrote, and I understand how you're feeling. Trust me, you're not the only one.

Let me start by assuring you that my Father and I have everything under control. Do you remember an old friend of ours named Job? I tell you, that guy went through more hardship and heartache than anybody I've known. He was a wealthy man when disaster struck. Much of his property was destroyed. His family was decimated, and he suffered through some terrible health problems. Like you, he worried about his future. His wife and friends offered advice--some of it good, some of it not so good. My father had to remind him of a few things. I'll do the same for you.

When worries pop into your head, remember this: My father and I framed the world at the beginning of time. We placed the stars in the sky. We designed the continents and filled the oceans. We created all the animals that populate the earth and gave each of them what they needed to survive. Even the smallest sparrow flying around your back yard does not escape our attention.

The sun comes up each morning on our command. We order the clouds to form and the rain to fall when it's dry. We make the farmers' crops grow so that you'll have food to eat. We personally design each snowflake that falls in the Midwest. We schedule the changes of season and maintain control over *everything*.

I have good news for you, Dan. Through faith, our old friend Job weathered all the storms that blew into his life. You will too. We have *great* things in store for you, so you can stop worrying!

Lots of love, Jesus

Dear Lord, When I worry today, remind me that you are in control of everything that happens to me. Help me to trust your will for my life. In Jesus' name, Amen.

Suggested Bible Reading: Matthew 10:28-31

My Thoughts

V is for Vicarious

I Corinthians 15:57 - But thanks be to God! He gives us the victory through our Lord Jesus Christ.

Hey, sports fans! How's it going? Has your team been winning? Has your favorite player been on top of his game? Have you seen him lately? Talked to him? Been invited over to his house? Didn't think so.

As a kid, I followed the Minnesota Vikings. I had posters of Gene Washington, Allan Page and Paul

Krause on my wall. I collected football cards of all the top players on the team. I wore the same beat up Vikings sweatshirt year 'round. Even the garbage can I kept in my bedroom had pictures of the Vikings' 22 starters from 1972. During backyard football games in the fall I pretended I was Fran Tarkenton scrambling out of the pocket or Chuck Foreman spinning away from tacklers. I knew as much as anybody about those guys.

The highlight of our year came when my dad took my brother and sister and me to Mankato to watch the Vikings practice. We would stand outside the locker room after practice hoping to catch a glimpse of the players and coaches. Once in a while a player would stop to sign an autograph or say hi, but most of them ignored us. It never dawned on me that I was not as important to them as they were to me.

Fans have followed sports teams and lived vicariously through their star players for as long as organized sports have existed. When the Astros win a World Series or the Patriots win another Super Bowl or the Warriors win an NBA title, entire cities revel in their teams' accomplishments. Many a fan will rationalize, "Since *my* team won the title, that makes *me* a champion!"

News flash! Your sports hero doesn't care about you. He has no idea who you are or where you live or what you're like. He cares about his next fat contract or commercial endorsement. He cares about the attention he gets when he travels and plays. He cares about himself.

Jesus presents a complete and absolute study in contrasts. From the very beginning of eternity, he cared about you. From the moment you were born he cared about you. When he lived here on earth, he was not concerned about where he lived or what he wore or what he ate. He was concerned about you. Today, from heaven, he cares about you.

How else can you explain what the Apostle Paul wrote in I Corinthians 15? That Christ died for our sins according to the Scriptures, that he was buried, that he was raised on the third day.

God allowed his Son to be put to death in order to save you from sin. He raised him from death on Easter morning to show that the payment for your sin was acceptable. God gave Jesus' victory over sin and death to you.

If your sports team wins a championship this year, go ahead and celebrate. Just remember that your sports heroes are in it for themselves. Your Savior, on the other hand, endured death on a cross so that you can be a champion forever.

Dear Lord, I know that you lived and died for me. You gave me the victory over death. Help me live for you today. In Jesus' name, Amen.

Suggested Bible Reading: Psalm 60

My Thoughts

W is for Wages

Romans 6:23 – For the wages of sin is death, but the gift of God is eternal life in Christ Jesus our Lord.

I worked hard when I was a kid. I was pragmatic about it. In other words, I always did work so that I would get something in return. On Saturday mornings I had to complete a list of chores for my mom and dad. When the chores were completed, I could go outside and play with my friends.

In third grade I 'walked beans' for a farmer in

Minnesota. I pulled velvet weeds from his fields for $1.50 an hour. It wasn't a lot of money, but the lunches that his wife made for us made up for it! In fourth grade I got a paper route. I delivered 35 papers after school every day to people in my neighborhood. I saved up enough money from delivering papers to buy my first bike, a beautiful green Schwinn stingray that cost $69.

In sixth grade I started working for a farmer in southern Wisconsin. I helped him bale hay, milk cows, clean barns and harvest tobacco. He paid me $3.00 an hour and 'straightened up' with me every couple weeks when he remembered his checkbook. For 21 years I taught school and coached basketball. I received a monthly paycheck that I used to pay my bills and take care of my family.

Every job I ever held paid some sort of wages. You could argue that work has intrinsic value—that working for work's sake is a commendable idea. If somebody offered me a job and said that I should be happy to work because working is noble, I would decline. I would find somebody who was willing to pay me wages for the work I did.

Reading Romans 6 got me thinking about some of the jobs I held over the years. However, the wages that Paul wrote about in v. 23 are different from the wages to which I referred. Wages connected with work are always negotiable.

The wages to which Paul refers are not. They aren't connected to a job. Rather, they are the direct result of a condition. That condition, of course, is sin. Every baby born of sinful parents is infected with a sinful nature. There's nothing you can do to avoid it. You can't quit sinning. You can't change bodies. You can't ignore your condition and hope it goes away. Paul's message is blunt. *The wages of sin is death.*

Thankfully, the last part of v. 23 offers great hope and comfort. *The gift of God is eternal life in Christ Jesus our Lord.* It's not unusual for an employer to give workers a bonus. It might be some extra money or a day of paid vacation. It might be a compliment on a job well done. The gift of God is unlike any bonus you will ever receive.

Eternal life isn't given to you because you worked hard or did something special. On the contrary, it is given to you because of the redemptive work of Jesus Christ, your Savior.

Dear Lord, I know the wages for my sin should be death. Thank you for giving me life instead. In Jesus' name, Amen.

Suggested Bible Reading: John 3:36

My Thoughts

X is for Excellence

Philippians 4:8 - Finally, brothers, whatever is true, whatever is noble, whatever is right, whatever is pure, whatever is lovely, whatever is admirable—if anything is excellent or praiseworthy—think about such things.

Excellence is always an option. I shared that scrap of wisdom with my students and my own children more times than I can count. Too often it seemed they would strive for mediocrity, or even less if possible. They often seemed to take pride in being moderately successful. They reveled in the joys of being average.

Every so often one of them would surprise me. I remember a handful of carefully researched, well-written research papers. I recall some artwork done by seventh graders that could have been hung in a museum. There were some heroic efforts put forth by my basketball teams. All too often, however, I was underwhelmed by middle-of-the-road, run-of-the-mill, ordinary effort.

If you haven't read Philippians 4 lately, I would encourage you to do it right now. It will help you appreciate the single verse listed above. Paul's letter to the church in Philippi was a plea to the congregation members to rejoice in their salvation. Along with rejoicing, he urged them to pursue lives of excellence.

In keeping with the positive spin of his message, Paul didn't mention anything about avoiding things that are false, ignoble, wrong, filthy, ugly, or unworthy. He wanted his listeners to think about and do praiseworthy things. Like me, he wanted his people to understand that excellence is always an option.

It's a good thing that Jesus understood this concept better than anyone. Think what might have happened if Jesus had been a moderately skilled teacher, a mediocre minister or an average

Savior. He would have told stories that had no hidden spiritual meanings. He likely would have preached sermons that put his listeners to sleep. He could have easily given up on his plan of redemption when the Roman soldiers beat him senseless.

Instead, Jesus' parables were flawless. Each story he told had practical and spiritual value. His sermons were brilliant. Each of them was filled with simple truths designed to increase the faith of his listeners. His plan of redemption was revolutionary. He was perfect, yet he willingly suffered the consequences for the sins of the whole world.

Truth? Fairness? Nobility? Righteousness? Purity? Loveliness? Our world has plenty of examples for us to think about. Our Savior Jesus Christ completely embodies every one of them. For him, excellence was the only option.

Dear Lord, You never settled for average. Everything you did was perfect. Help me strive for excellence today in all that I do. In Jesus' name. Amen.

Suggested Bible Reading: Matthew 5:48

My Thoughts

Y is for *You*

John 3:16 – For God so loved the world that he gave his one and only son, that whoever believes in him will not perish but have eternal life.

Try wrapping your mind around these numbers. Some scientists estimate the size of our universe to be 156 billion light-years wide. The speed of light is 186,000 miles per second. One light-year is the distance light can travel in a year. Try doing the math. The numbers are so huge they stagger the imagination. Despite the seemingly infinite size of the universe, God loves *you*!

The Milky Way, the galaxy where earth resides, is one of millions of galaxies dispersed throughout the universe. The planets in our solar system revolve around the sun, a medium-sized yellow dwarf star. Don't let the word *dwarf* fool you. The sun is still 1.3 million times larger than earth. No matter how vast our solar system, God loves *you*!

Planet earth is the only place discovered so far that can sustain life. The circumference of the earth is 24,900 miles and it weighs approximately 13,200,000,000,000,000,000,000,000 pounds. As of August 2019, there were about 7.66 billion human beings living on earth. Even though you are just one person in a sea of humanity, God loves *you*!

The country in which you live is 3,400 miles from coast to coast at its widest part and inhabited by over 328 million people. These people have come from all 195 countries around the world. They come in all shapes, sizes, and colors. Even though you are just one of 328 million, God loves *you*!

The school you attend could have anywhere from 20 to 2,000 students. Your classroom is most likely home to 25 to 30 kids. At times, you might get lost in the shuffle. Keep your chin up; God loves *you*!

Your family unit most likely has two to six people in it. It's possible you are the youngest child in the family. There might be times when you feel that nobody cares who you are, what you're doing, or where you're going. Stay cheerful. God loves *you*!

It's true. In the scope of the universe, you are just a tiny speck. On the world's stage, you are a minor player. In your school, you're probably just average. In your family, you may be the least gifted. None of that matters! God made you exactly how he wanted you to be. He knit you together in your mother's womb. He numbered the hairs on your head. He knows every feeling, thought and desire in your heart and mind.

For God so loved *you* that he gave his one and only son. If *you* believe in him, *you* will not perish. *You* will have eternal life.

Dear Lord, I know I am just one person in this vast universe. Thank you for loving me and watching out for me anyway! In Jesus' name, Amen.

Suggested Bible Reading: I John 4:12

My Thoughts

_____
_____
_____
_____
_____
_____
_____
_____
_____
_____
_____
_____
_____
_____
_____
_____
_____
_____
_____
_____
_____

Z is for Zealous

Galatians 4:18a - It is fine to be zealous, provided the purpose is good.

A recent article in our local newspaper caught my eye. It featured six local people who had changed religions. One man who served for years as a Catholic priest had become a secular humanist and abandoned his faith in God. A female member of the United Church of Christ had converted to Judaism. A former agnostic had become a Baptist.

The features were a little short on details that

could explain the conversions, but I suspect a couple of things happened. First, each person must have become disillusioned with whatever religious beliefs he or she had once learned. Second, each most likely came in contact with a person from a different religious background that was zealous enough in his or her beliefs to encourage change.

Paul, the Apostle, remains a classic example of a dramatic conversion. Most readers of this book know the story. Paul zealously worked against the early Christian church, believing in his heart that the followers of Jesus were an affront to his traditional Jewish beliefs. God personally confronted Paul and changed his heart. He then set Paul on a lifetime journey of international mission work that would change the ancient religious world.

I won't point fingers because of my own hang-ups, but allow me to ask you a question. What are you zealous about? Never missing your favorite weekly television show? Following your favorite sports team? Improving your high score on a video game? Keeping your room clean? (Ok, forget that last one.)

There's nothing wrong with any of those things. However, they really shouldn't take priority over your faith life. Why not be zealous about going to church on Sunday? Why not be zealous about regularly studying God's word by yourself or with others? Why not be zealous about communicating with God in prayer every day? Why not be zealous about sharing *your* faith?

It would have been nice to see one of those converts tell about his or her conversion to the Lutheran-Christian faith. It would have been nice to hear a story about how a neighbor influenced one of the subjects of the article to start attending church and to have his children baptized.

It would have been encouraging to learn that, because of the influence of a neighbor zealous about his Christian faith, the eternal course of a soul had been changed for the better.

Dear Lord, There are times when I don't feel zealous about being a Christian. Change my attitude and help me be excited about sharing my love for you. In Jesus' name, Amen.

Suggested Bible Reading: Galatians 4:12-17

My Thoughts

*B*onus Section

Practical Applications of God's 10 ~~Suggestions~~ Commandments for Young Christians

*U*nderstanding and Obedience
The 1st Commandment

You shall have no other gods.
What does this mean?
**We should fear, love and trust
in God above all things.**

Consider me your new compliance officer for the time it takes you to work through these next 11 articles.

All major college athletic departments have compliance officers. Their main job is to make sure administrators, coaches, and players understand and obey the rules as they pertain to interscholastic competition. Sounds simple until you consider the current manual of rules and regulations is 427 pages long. My guess is that not a single coach or player has ever read the entire manual or understands half of what's in it. That responsibility falls to the compliance office.

The NCAA puts lots of rules in place to make sure schools compete fairly with each other. If coaches or players break the rules, punishments can be harsh. One former example should suffice. While there are new NCAA violations every year, here is one example of rules gone wrong. Kelvin Sampson used to be the head coach for the University of Oklahoma men's basketball program. He was forced to leave that position when it was discovered he had broken some recruiting rules. He and his staff had made hundreds of illegal phone calls to potential high school recruits. Strangely enough, the University of Indiana hired him as their head coach shortly after he left Oklahoma. At Indiana, Sampson committed the same violations and was forced to resign in disgrace. Both programs faced severe punishments, and it's unlikely Sampson will ever coach college basketball again.

God's list of rules for you to follow is summarized in the Ten Commandments. He issued these ten commands to Moses and expected His Old Testament followers to obey them. All ten are still in play today. God did not give you rules to follow to burden your existence or suck the fun out of your life. He gave them to protect you, your property, and your family.

The First Commandment protects the relationship you have with God. One of the reasons God created you in the first place was to position you in a unique relationship with Him. He loves you and provides for you. He protects you, forgives you, and grants you eternal salvation. In turn, He expects total devotion from your heart, mind, and soul through fearing, loving, and trusting Him above all things.

It's unusual in human relationships to fear, love, and trust the same person. You can fear a person without loving him. You can love a person without trusting him. You can trust a person without fearing him.

Because of our natural inclination to sin, it's not possible for us to fear, love, and trust God perfectly. If it we could do this, there would be no need for any other commandments. Thankfully, Jesus is our compliance officer. Jesus kept God's Law. He perfectly feared, loved, and trusted God in our place. He also put us in compliance with God's justice by dying for our sins. As believing children, we thank Jesus for His forgiveness and ask Him to help us fear, love and trust in God above all things.

*P*ray, Praise, and Give Thanks
The 2nd Commandment

You shall not take the name of the
Lord, your God, in vain.
What does this mean?
We should fear and love God, so that
we do not curse, swear, practice
witchcraft, lie or deceive by His name,
but call upon Him in every trouble,
pray, praise, and give thanks.

If you were expecting a standard lecture about using God's name carelessly, spewing foul language, fooling around with the occult, lying, etc., I'm sorry to disappoint you.

As a Christian boy or girl, man or woman, you know those things are wrong. You know even though sins against the Second Commandment often seem small in the eyes of men, they are great before God. Finally, you know Jesus kept this commandment perfectly in thought, word, and deed on your behalf.

Instead, I'd like to encourage you to heed the three action words in the title of this column—pray, praise, and give thanks.

Pray for yourself. Pray that God would reveal his will for you in your life. Pray that he would protect you physically, emotionally, and spiritually. Pray that he would forgive your sins each day. Pray that your football team wins on Sunday if you want.

Pray for others. Pray for members of your family. Pray for members of your church. Pray for your friends. Pray for your teachers and pastors. Pray for the leaders of your country. Pray for your dog if you want.

Praise God the Father for creating the world in which you live. Praise him for designing you as a unique individual. Praise him for the gifts and abilities he has given you. Praise him for knowing you better than you know yourself.

Praise God the Son for being your Savior from sin. Praise him for setting a perfect example of behavior. Praise him for promising to take you to heaven to spend eternity with him.

Praise God the Holy Spirit for giving you faith. Praise him for living in your heart and helping you understand God's word. Praise him for giving you the courage to share the message of the Gospel with other people.

Give thanks for your home, your clothes, and your food. Give thanks for the friendships you have at school or work. Give thanks for your mom and dad, your grandparents, your aunts, uncles, and cousins. Give thanks for your brothers and sisters. Give thanks for your health, your freedoms, and your opportunities.

Use God's name the way it was intended!

*T*ime for Church!
The 3rd Commandment

You shall keep the day of rest holy.
What does this mean?
**We should fear and love God so that
we do not despise preaching and his
word, but hold it sacred and gladly
hear and learn it.**

I can't pinpoint the exact time in my life when I started to enjoy going to church. Since my father was a pastor, and since we lived close to the churches he served, I *had* to go to church all the time. It didn't matter how late I stayed up or if I wasn't feeling well or if I didn't want to go. On

Sunday mornings I got a wake-up call from my mom and was expected to be in the pew next to her by the time the church bells rang.

So I went. Sometimes under extreme duress. Every Sunday. Midweek Lenten services. Special services at Thanksgiving, Christmas, and New Year's. Weddings. Funerals.

My appreciation for and attention to worship were at times appalling.

Things have changed. I love going to church now. I look forward to each worship service. I enjoy keeping the day of rest holy, whether it's Sunday morning, Monday evening, or another day of the week.

It's not because we have a new church building in a bucolic setting surrounded by beautiful oak trees. It's not because the worship times happen to fit our schedule. It's not because our pastor has a knack for explaining scripture. It's not because the members of our church are friendly and supportive of each other. It's not because the snacks in the lobby are tasty and the coffee is better than average.

I look forward to going to church because I need to hear two things on a regular basis.

First, I need to be reminded that I'm a sinner. If I go too long without standing before the mirror of God's law, it's easy to start thinking I'm not so bad. It's easy to compare myself to my jerky neighbor and think I'm better than him. It's easy to forget what a wretched sinner I am and that on my own I would be doomed.

Second, I need to hear the Gospel. If I go too long without the reassuring message of forgiveness and salvation, it's easy to despair. I need to hear that God loves me with a perfect, holy, everlasting love. I need to hear that all my sins are forgiven because of the debt Jesus paid. I need to be reminded that I have a place in heaven waiting for me when I die.

I'm looking forward to the next day of rest!

*T*he Benefits of Obedience
The 4th Commandment

Honor your father and mother, that it may be well with you, and that you may live long on the earth.
What does this mean?
We should fear and love God, so that we do not despise our parents and superiors, nor provoke them to anger, but honor, serve, obey, love and esteem them.

Listen to your parents. Live to be 95! Makes sense, doesn't it? Not so fast. The condition attached to the 4th Commandment should include a couple of disclaimers.

Firstly, the inferred promise of a long life had roots in Old Testament civil and ceremonial laws. These laws had specific application to the nation of Israel as they prepared to enter the Promised Land. Though the moral application of the 4th Commandment is binding today, the civil and ceremonial applications are not.

Secondly, despite your best intentions, you will never be able to keep the 4th Commandment perfectly. Sorry. For every time you served your parents, there were a hundred times when you made their lives more difficult. For every time you showed them honor, there were a hundred times you made them wish they had a different last name. For every time you made them happy and proud, there were a hundred times you angered or disappointed them.

When you examine your relationship with your parents and others that God placed over you, Jesus' perfect obedience to earthly authorities becomes all the more remarkable. He never talked back. He never disobeyed. He never harbored thoughts of hatred when he was chastised. Best of all, he obeyed his heavenly Father and went to the cross to pay for the sins of all people.

Showing obedience, honor and respect to your parents and others in authority does have an upside.

Think back to some of the directions your parents gave you when you were younger. If your mom and dad are anything like mine, I'm guessing you heard many of the same things I heard. Nearly every suggestion had ramifications relative to a long, healthy life.

Look both ways before crossing the street. Drink your milk and eat your vegetables. Be nice to your brothers and sisters. Get lots of exercise. Choose your friends carefully. Don't drive too fast. Work hard at your job. Spend your money wisely. Don't use illegal substances.

Generally speaking, submitting to God's will through obedience to your parents will make you less susceptible to sinful stresses that can shorten life.

In the end, it's important to understand the actual intent of the 4th Commandment regardless of the original inferred promise. You are to model obedience to your parents and others in authority so that God will be obeyed.

*T*he Spirit of the Law
The 5th Commandment

You shall not kill.
What does this mean?
**We should fear and love God, so that
we do no bodily harm to our neighbor,
but help and befriend him in every
need.**

Killing is big business these days. Movies that
glorify sadistic killers rake in millions at the box
office. Violent video games allow players to mow

down virtual enemies with an array of supercharged weapons. People who enjoy these things justify them as fun—nothing more than fantasy, an escape from the real world. Detractors of these products argue that, despite their fantasy component, they degrade human life.

There is a fine line between the letter of the law and the spirit of the law. The letter of the law relative to the 5th Commandment is clear. You shall not kill. God does not sanction the taking of another person's life except in a couple of extreme situations.

The spirit of the law relative to Luther's explanation is more appealing to discuss here. We are encouraged to help and befriend our neighbor in every need. With that in mind, I have a story to share about my neighbor.

My next-door neighbor and his family don't attend church. He and I have become very close friends over the years. I love him and his family. I've invited him many times to visit our church with us, and he has always declined. A number of years ago on a Saturday afternoon I asked him if he might want to go to church the next day. To my surprise he said, "Sure. I don't have anything going on. We'll all go." The next morning he and his wife and two young children hopped in our car and we went to church together.

I think they enjoyed the experience. Their four-year-old son got restless toward the end of the sermon. I took him out into the narthex and colored with him for a bit. Our pastor preached a great sermon, and we welcomed two new members into our congregation.

The next day I sent him an email that explained a few things about the Lutheran church. He responded by saying that he appreciated the invite and valued our friendship.

I've broken the 5th Commandment countless times. Only Jesus' perfect obedience to this commandment covers my mistakes. But in this instance I adhered to both the letter *and* the spirit of the law. A.) I didn't kill my neighbor. B.) I helped and befriended him by sharing the Gospel of our Savior.

Disregard for human life may be big business these days, but life everlasting remains the focus of God's children.

*F*or Better or Worse
The 6th Commandment

You shall not commit adultery.
What does this mean?
**We should fear and love God, so that we lead
a chaste and decent life in word and deed,
and that husband and wife each love and
honor the other.**

Of all the things that disappoint God about sinful human beings, their treatment of the institution of marriage must rank near the top.

God always intended for marriage to be a life-long commitment. Today, half of all marriages in the

U.S. end in divorce. God intended marriage to be a special union between a male and a female. Today, forces who oppose traditional marriage are clamoring for the rights of people to marry members of their own sex. God intended marriage to serve as a vehicle for producing and rearing children. Today, millions of children are born out of wedlock.

My wife and I will be married 39 years this September. Ours is not a perfect marriage, but it is still a marriage. Despite selfish interests, occasional disagreements and differing views, we have a Christ-centered relationship. We love each other and enjoy spending time together. I can't speak for my wife, but I'm thankful she is my spouse!

In a short column like this, I couldn't begin to plumb the depths of resources available that address marriage and relationship building. I can share one piece of solid advice, however, and it would be this: Put the needs of your boyfriend, girlfriend or spouse ahead of your own. Simple, right? In theory, yes. In practice, no.

One of the most remarkable traits of human behavior is the desire for physical and emotion self-preservation. In a relationship with the opposite sex, especially in the confines of marriage, that desire often manifests itself in one quality—selfishness.

Think of how often you or say, "I want!" or "I need!" If you consistently place your own wants and needs ahead of those of your boyfriend, girlfriend or spouse, you can expect plenty of strife. When you put the needs of others ahead of your own, you'll be amazed at how fulfilling your relationships can be.

The best model of selflessness has always been Jesus Christ. In his relationships with friends and coworkers, he always put their needs ahead of his own. In his personal relationship with you and me, that remarkable trait is always on display. I know that he always has my best interests at heart. He gives me good food, comfortable housing, and ample clothing. He forgives my sins every single day. He has already prepared a place in heaven for me to dwell.

Modeling Christ's selfless behavior is a great way to strengthen relationships!

Go Ahead and Ask!
The 7th Commandment

You shall not steal.
What does this mean?
We should fear and love God, so that
we do not take our neighbor's money
or goods, nor get them in any dishonest
way, but help him to improve and
protect his goods and means of making
a living.

You can steal a kiss, steal some time alone or steal

a nap and not be in violation of the 7th Commandment. Rather, God's command not to steal is related to wrongful acquisition of another person's property. It could take an hour to describe the meaning of the word 'property' and another hour to explain all the different methods of stealing. Suffice it to say, when you take what does not rightly belong to you with the intent of keeping it, you are stealing.

I would suggest that in many cases stealing is the symptom of a bigger problem—lack of trust in God's provision.

Like any good father, God provides for all of his children. The amount and variety of property that God provides varies from person to person. In James 4, the writer addresses discontent that could lead to stealing, "What causes fights and quarrels among you? Don't they come from the desires that battle within you? You want something but don't get it. You kill and covet, but you cannot have what you want."

Without going into my private, personal history of petty larceny, I can assure you that I have been guilty of the discontent described by James that leads to stealing.

If stealing happens to be a pet sin, I would offer a couple of suggestions: First, ask God to forgive you for past transgressions of the 7th Commandment. Jesus has paid for every sin of stealing you ever paid for every sin of stealing you ever committed. In effect, he stole the guilt of your sin and took it to the cross.

Second, ask God to help you be content with what you have. James continues in chapter 4 by saying, "When you ask, you do not receive, because you ask with wrong motives." God wants you to ask for things. When he grants your request, be thankful! When he doesn't, remember that godliness with contentment is great gain.

You can steal someone's heart or steal away from a crowd of people without breaking the 7th Commandment. In the end, you brought nothing into the world, and you can take nothing out of it!

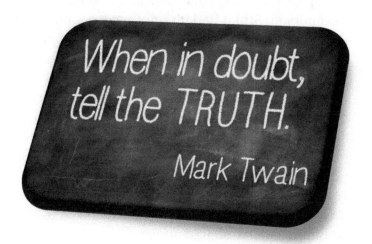

The Source of Truth
The 8th Commandment

You shall not bear false witness against your neighbor.
What does this mean?
We should fear and love God so that we do not lie about, betray or slander our neighbor, but excuse him, speak well of him and put the best construction on everything.

Truth means something to followers of Christ. I appreciate a well-researched, factual, interesting newspaper or magazine article as much as the next person. Still, I find it tempting every now and then to peruse the tabloids that populate supermarket checkout racks and airport kiosks. There's something about Zac Efron's abs, Kim Kardashian's love life and Miley Cyrus' wardrobe that I find absurdly fascinating. Purveyors of this sort of literature walk a fine line between obedience and disobedience to the 8th Commandment. Each of us ought to observe respect for the private lives of other people, including celebrities. People in charge of communications should maintain a fair balance between what the public needs to know and respect for an individual's right to privacy and freedom.

My point? Followers of Christ respect the truth!

The Bible attests to the fact that God is the source of all truth. His word is truth. His law is truth, and in Jesus Christ His truth became manifest. It's part of human nature to seek the truth, especially when it comes to spiritual matters. The 8th Commandment urges truthfulness when it comes to dealing with your neighbor—*do not lie about, betray or slander your neighbor, but excuse him, speak well of him and put the best construction on everything*. That beautiful, rhythmic phrase from Luther's Small Catechism should be posted at the entrance to all neighborhoods. Truthfulness, sincerity and candor are virtues that allow you to live in harmony with others and serve as guards against duplicity, dishonesty and hypocrisy.

My point? Followers of Christ live in the truth!

When Jesus stood before Pilate, he said, "For this reason I was born, and for this I came into the world, to testify to the truth. Everyone on the side of truth listens to me." Jesus' disciples, for the most part, understood this in their own lives. The majority of them suffered martyrdom, the supreme act of witnessing to the truth. Today, when Christians find themselves in situations that require witnessing, they ought to profess their faith without hesitation.

My point? Followers of Christ bear witness to the truth!

God's command to 'not bear false witness against our neighbor' carries some additional weight when the concept of truthfulness is added to the equation. Suffice it to say again: Truth means something to followers of Christ.

*T*iny Houses
The 9th Commandment

You shall not covet your neighbor's house.
What does this mean?
We should fear and love God so that we do not craftily seek to gain our neighbor's inheritance or home, nor get it by a show or right, but help and serve him in keeping it.

There was a time when I was guilty of coveting my neighbor's house for the simple reason that my wife and I couldn't afford to buy one. After getting married we lived in two different apartments.

Eventually we rented a small, single-story home that my father-in-law had purchased. Like a lot of young couples, we dreamed of owning our own home but couldn't afford it. After I had been teaching for a couple of years we decided to go house hunting. A realtor reviewed our finances and took us to look at some houses he thought we could afford. It was a humiliating experience. The places he showed us were barely fit for human habitation.

The time came when we were blessed with the means to build our own home in Wisconsin and buy a second home in Florida. Owning one property is a lot of responsibility; owning two doubled the fun. Our three kids are grown and gone and now, instead of coveting our neighbor's house because we don't have one, we have *too* much house and would like to downsize.

I remember getting an email from a friend about a guy who builds tiny houses. No kidding! They're really tiny! The house featured in this video was 90 square feet, about the size of the closet in our master bedroom. The builder wanted to simply his life and reduce living expenses. He designed every square inch to be functional. The frame sits on wheels so he can hitch it to his truck and move it wherever he wants to go. His utility bill for the whole year came to $89! Apparently there are a lot of people interested in this concept because he started getting requests from around the country to design and build more and now runs a business doing just that.

Question #83 in Luther's Small Catechism says, "Of what does our earthly home or place to live remind us?" Allow me to refresh your memory. Our earthly home or place to live (whether large or tiny) reminds us of the heavenly inheritance or home which Jesus has prepared for us.

Think about this fact: In heaven there will be no mortgage payments, no property taxes, no utility bills, no broken air conditioner compressors, no TV repairs, no hurricane insurance, no garage to clean, no lawn to mow, no garbage disposals to replace, no carpets to clean and no windows to wash.

We'll have uninterrupted communication with our creator, constant companionship with our Savior Jesus, flawless understanding of the Holy Spirit, perfect bodies, brilliant minds, sinless hearts, joyful reunions with our loved ones and an eternity of bliss and happiness.

That's something worth coveting!

*D*esire Gone Wrong
The 10th Commandment

You shall not covet your neighbor's wife, nor his manservant, nor his maidservant, nor his cattle, nor anything that is his.
What does this mean?
We should fear and love god, so that we do not tempt, force or coax away from our neighbor his wife or his workers, but urge them to stay and do their duty.

English proverb: "The grass is always greener on the other side of the fence.'

Scottish saying: 'A covetous man won't have enough until his mouth is filled with mold.'

In a nutshell, coveting is desire gone wrong. Understand, desire allows doctors to cure diseases; desire propels football teams to championships; desire helps business leaders build companies. But desire gone wrong causes embarrassment—just ask King David. Desire gone wrong leads to death and destruction—just ask Absalom. Desire gone wrong leads to betrayal—just ask Judas.

It's ok to desire a pet, a car, good grades, a boyfriend, a girlfriend, a wife, money, etc. It's wrong to desire these things when they belong to somebody else. If you're like me, you can remember a time when you coveted something, took steps to acquire it and then felt utterly disappointed and unfulfilled with whatever it was you had gotten. That pitiful loop has no doubt played and replayed throughout your life.

Covetousness begins quietly in the heart. It's like a defect in your steering mechanism. If left unchecked, it can pull you out of alignment. It will steal, injure or destroy to get what it wants. Covetousness will never be fully satisfied.

Learning to overcome covetousness also begins in the heart, a heart that has submitted to God's will and God's rules. Matthew didn't write, 'Seek first the kingdom of things.' He wrote, 'Seek first the kingdom of God and his righteousness, and all these things will be given to you as well.'

I dare you to put God to the test in that regard. Keep in mind that you already are in possession of the greatest treasure known to man. By faith you have an abundance of riches that will never spoil or be taken away.

The change of heart that conquers covetousness began with your baptism. It continues with daily repentance and forgiveness. It will conclude with the fulfillment of God's promise to take you to heaven.

Good News Cannot be Hidden
The Conclusion to the 10 Commandments

I, the Lord your God, am a jealous God, punishing the children for the sin of the fathers to the third and fourth generation of those who hate me, but showing love to a thousand generations of those who love me and keep my commandments.

What does this mean?

God threatens to punish all who break these commandments. Therefore, we should fear His wrath and not do anything against them. But He promises grace and every blessing to all who keep these commandments. Therefore, we should also love and trust in Him and gladly do what He commands.

Picture the start of a three-legged race. Kids' legs are tied together. Pairs of giggling runners struggle to the starting line, trying to find balance with their partners. As soon as the race starts, you can bet that half the participants will stumble and fall. However, once the runners figure out how to work in sync with each other, they can really fly!

Let's start (and end) with this scriptural truth: God wants all people to be saved and to come to a knowledge of the truth. After Adam and Eve sinned, God promised to send a Savior. His son Jesus answered the call, fulfilled the Law and died for the sins of the entire world.

Don't forget, God is also interested in you and your life. His personal relationship with you is paramount! He watches you as you go to school. He cares about who you choose as friends. He listens to your public conversations and is privy to your innermost thoughts and feelings. Bottom line? He wants you to walk in line with his will for your life, and that includes obedience to the 10 Commandments. When you struggle against God's will and go your own way, you'll stumble and fall like kids at the beginning of a three-legged race.

When I first read the conclusion to the Commandments, some serious questions popped into my head. Would I be punished for my father's sins? Would my kids be punished for mine? The answer? Let me be resoundingly clear! Jesus was punished for my father's sins. He was punished for my sins. He was punished for your sins. His perfect obedience to God's Law has been credited to your account! As a result of Jesus' redemptive work, God sees you as a perfect, righteous child who deserves forgiveness, life and salvation!

That Good News cannot be hidden. It cannot be overstated. It cannot be heard often enough!

Made in USA - Kendallville, IN
1062865_9781952037047
03.26.2020 0823